T0041771

# The Little Book of BAD MOODS

WRITTEN BY LOTTA SONNINEN

ILLUSTRATIONS BY PIIA AHO

GALLERY BOOKS

New York London Toronto Sydney New Delhi

Gallery Books
An Imprint of Simon & Schuster, Inc.
1230 Avenue of the Americas
New York, NY 10020

Copyright © 2018 by Lotta Sonninen
English-language translation copyright © 2018 by Lotta Sonninen
First published in 2018 in Finland by Otava Publishing as *Pieni pahan mielen kirja*. This English-language edition published by agreement with Lotta Sonninen and Elina Ahlback Literary Agency, Helsinki, Finland. First published in the United States in 2019. Cover, graphic design, and illustrations by Otava Publishing Company Ltd. / Piia Aho. Lotta Sonninen and Otava Publishing Company Ltd. /Piia Aho have asserted their right under the Copyright, Designs and Patents Act, 1988, to be identified as author and illustrator, respectively, of this work.

All rights reserved, including the right to reproduce this book or portions thereof in any form whatsoever. For information, address Gallery Books Subsidiary Rights Department, 1230 Avenue of the Americas, New York, NY 10020.

First Gallery Books hardcover edition February 2019

GALLERY BOOKS and colophon are registered trademarks of Simon & Schuster, Inc.

For information about special discounts for bulk purchases, please contact Simon & Schuster Special Sales at 1-866-506-1949 or business@simonandschuster.com.

The Simon & Schuster Speakers Bureau can bring authors to your live event. For more information or to book an event, contact the Simon & Schuster Speakers Bureau at 1-866-248-3049 or visit our website at www.simonspeakers.com.

Manufactured in the United States of America

10 9 8 7 6 5 4 3 2 1

Library of Congress Cataloging-in-Publication Data is available.

ISBN 978-1-9821-2262-1

## Contents


Blame others **6**

Name names **20**

Draw the line **26**

Channel your bitterness **34**

How to make any day a bad day **40**

Life sucks online **48**

No forgetting, no forgiving **58**

Find the bad in the world **72**

Badden your vocabulary **88**

Just say it already **98**

Color me bad **108**

Forecast is dismal **118**

BLAME

# OTHERS

List what's wrong with your spouse.

X

X

X

X

X

List what's wrong with your parents.

X

X

X

X

X

X

List what's wrong with your kids.

X

X

X

X

X

List what's wrong with your boss.

X

X

X

X

X

X

List what's wrong with your friends.

| NAME | FAULTS |
| --- | --- |
| | |

What former boss/colleague/employee of yours still makes you angry and why?

Which of your EXes do you still hate and why?

How do you spot an idiot **in the checkout line**?

How do you spot an idiot *walking down the street*?

How do you spot an idiot **IN A RESTAURANT**?

How do you spot an idiot **on a date**?

How do you spot an idiot
IN TRAFFIC?

How do you spot an idiot **TRAVELING ABROAD**?

How do you spot an idiot *online*?

How do you spot an idiot **AT WORK**?

Idiots I've met *at work*:

Idiots I've met IN TRAFFIC:

IDIOTS I'VE MET *on dates*:

Idiots I've met **at bars**:

Idiots I've met **THROUGH MY HOBBIES**:

Idiots I've met **online**:

## List *acquaintances* or *celebrities* who...

...have had it way too easy

X

X

X

X

...think too much of themselves

X

X

X

X

...have no idea what's best for them

X

X

X

X

...should just go back to school

X

X

X

X

...should think more before opening their mouths

X

X

X

X

The absolutely most annoying type of person is

Your boss's most irritating habit

Your spouse's most irritating habit

Your teacher's most irritating habit

Your child's most irritating habit

Your grandmother's most irritating habit

Your neighbor's most irritating habit

The most irritating thing about TV

The most irritating thing about politics

# NAME

# NAMES

What's wrong with your life?

WHAT'S WRONG

## WHOSE FAULT IS IT?

Make a list of people who are **less talented than you** but still *more successful.*

X

X

X

X

X

X

X

X

X

X

X

# I'M JEALOUS OF...

| NAME | REASON |
| --- | --- |
| | |

# DRAW THE LINE

Give this **voodoo doll** a face or other distinguishing features.

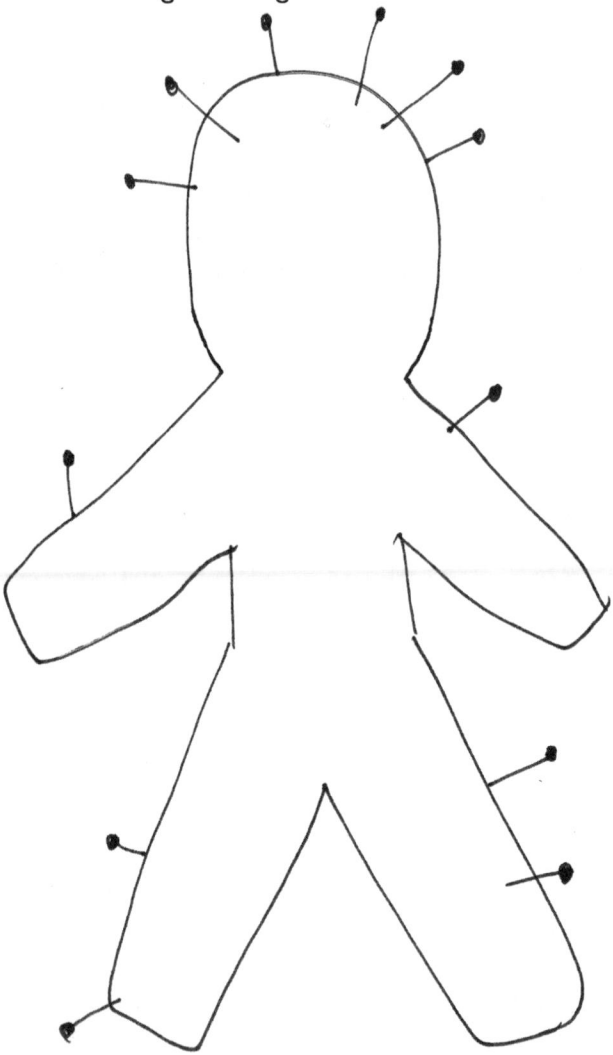

Draw an UGLY animal.

Draw and color

# AN UGLY OUTFIT.

Draw and color

# DISGUSTING FOOD.

Draw **a traffic sign**

that would forbid something you hate.

Design some ugly wallpaper.

# CHANNEL YOUR BITTERNESS

Think of three ways to irritate
**YOUR SPOUSE.**

-

-

-

Think of three ways to irritate
**YOUR PARENTS.**

-

-

-

Think of three ways to irritate
**YOUR COWORKERS.**

-

-

-

Think of three ways to irritate
**YOUR BOSS.**

-

-

-

Think of three ways to irritate
**YOUR FELLOW TRAVELERS.**

-

-

-

Think of three ways to be irritating
**ONLINE.**

-

-

-

# Fill in the blanks.

My life would be much easier if _____
wasn't so _____.

The world would be a much better place if _____
didn't always _____.

_____ can't even _____,
and yet he/she always _____.

I get bored out of my mind whenever _____
starts to talk about his/her _____.

The next time _____ starts to _____,
I'm going to lose it.

I have no idea why I ever _____ with _____.

I truly don't know why _____ was ever invented.

I don't understand why men always have to _____.

I don't understand why women always have to

_____.

I don't understand why kids always have to

_____.

I don't understand why _____ always has to _____.

It's the 21st century, for heaven's sake. Why do

_____ still _____?

If I'd known that _____, I never would have _____.

All _____ are idiots because they _____.

If I could decide, _____

would be forbidden from _____.

If I could decide, _____ would be

erased from the earth.

# HOW TO MAKE ANY DAY A BAD DAY

List what was wrong with this week.

| | I WAS ANNOYED BY | THIS RUINED THE DAY |
|---|---|---|
| Monday | | |
| Tuesday | | |
| Wednesday | | |
| | | |

| | Sunday | Saturday | Friday | Thursday |
|---|---|---|---|---|
| I WAS ANNOYED BY | | | | |
| THIS RUINED THE DAY | | | | |

## The Vacation of My
# NIGHTMARES

Place:

Company:

Schedule:

Menu:

The Christmas

# FROM HELL

Place:

Company:

Schedule:

Menu:

## Keep an ingratitude journal!

List everything that bothered you this week.

Monday I was annoyed by...

Tuesday I was annoyed by...

Wednesday I was annoyed by...

Thursday I was annoyed by...

Friday I was annoyed by...

Saturday I was annoyed by...

Sunday I was annoyed by...

# LIFE SUCKS

# ONLINE

Most infuriating status updates

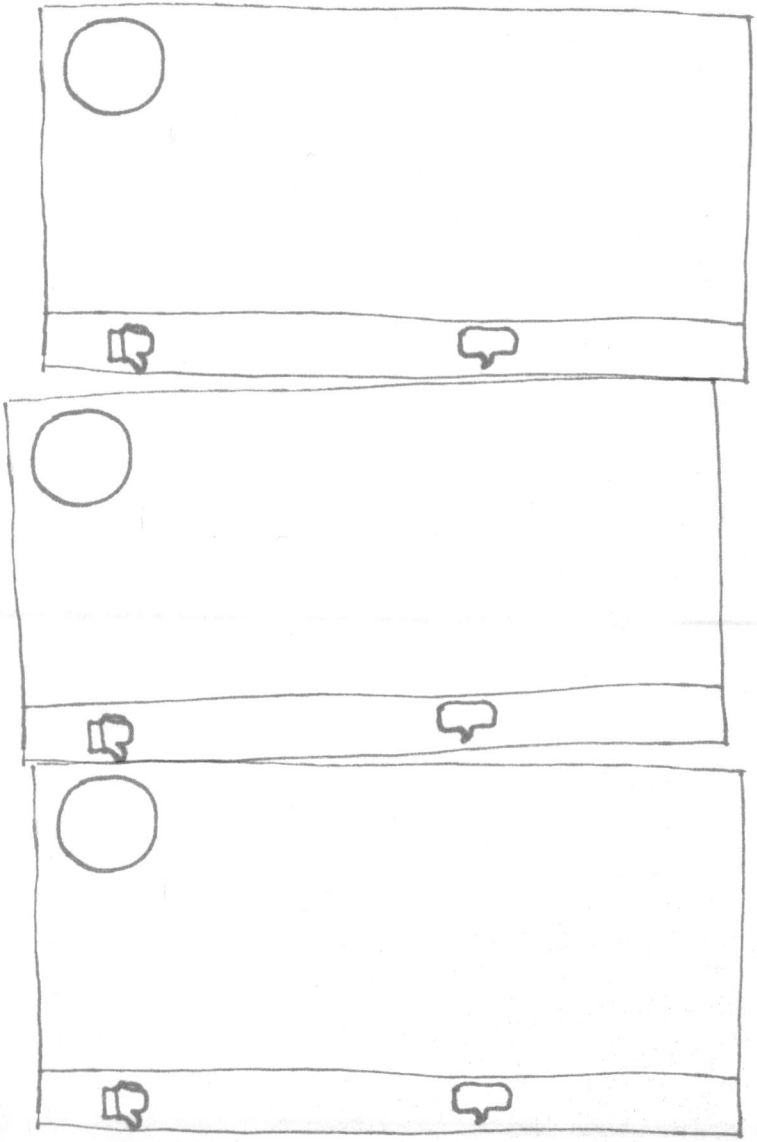

Stupidest blogs

Instacrap

Most birdbrained tweets

Emojis that need to be punched in the face

Worst computer trouble

Most incompetent IT support 

Draw new emojis
that express rage or frustration.

Use this space to write emails you wish you could send but won't ever dare.

Recipient:

CC:

Subject:

Message:

Recipient:

CC:

Subject:

Message:

Recipient:

CC:

Subject:

Message:

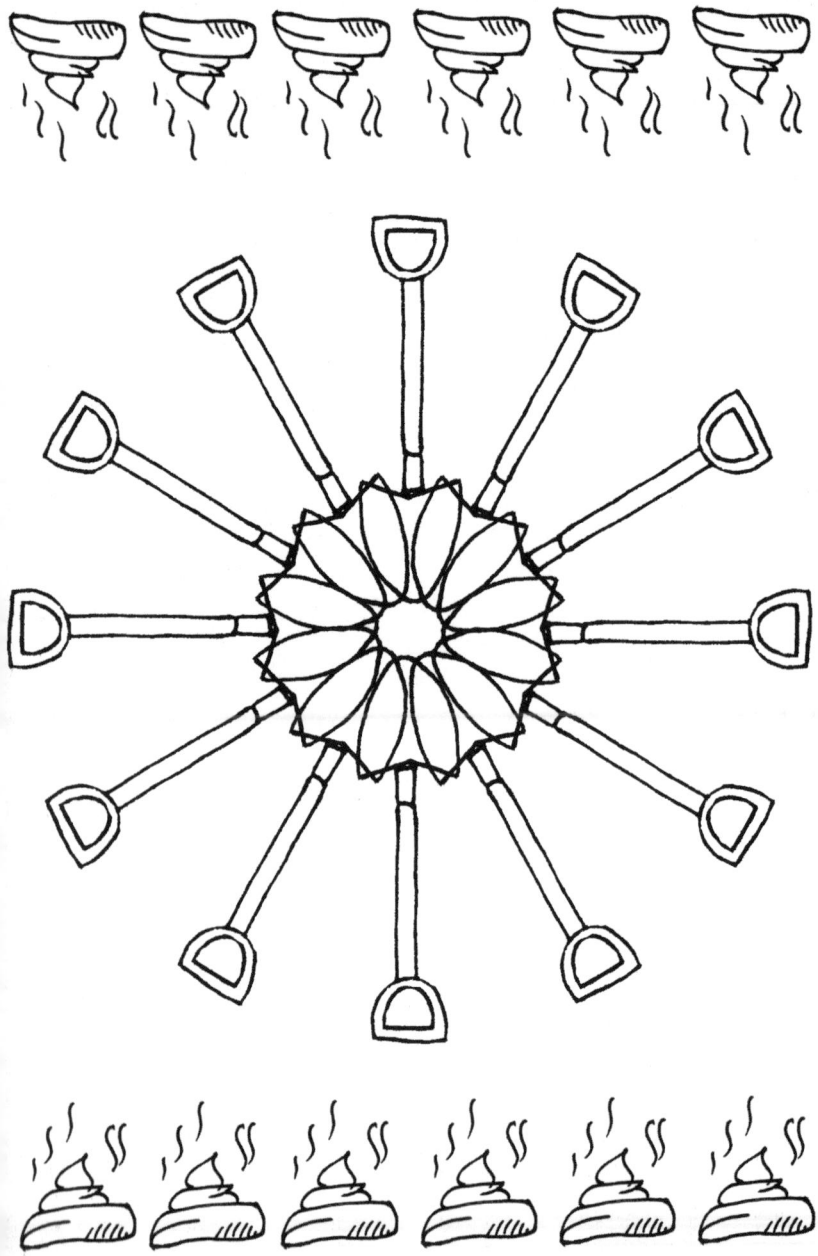

# NO FORGETTING

# NO FORGIVING

# I most **regret**...

# I'll **never** forgive...

# I'm STILL bitter about...

List situations where you didn't think of a **GOOD COMEBACK** until it was over.

| TIME, PLACE AND PEOPLE | PERFECT COMEBACK |
| --- | --- |
| | |
| | |
| | |
| | |
| | |

| TIME, PLACE AND PEOPLE | PERFECT COMEBACK |
| --- | --- |
| | |
| | |
| | |
| | |
| | |

Worst **VACATION DISASTER**

Worst **RELATIONSHIP DISASTER**

Worst *purchase disaster*

Worst HAIR DISASTER

Worst outfit disaster

Worst party disaster

Worst COOKING DISASTER

Worst CHILDHOOD DISASTER

Worst school memory

Worst SCHOOL FOOD memory

Worst personal hygiene memory

Worst doctor's office memory

Worst *dentist visit* memory

Worst **ONLINE** memory

Worst **DATE** memory

Worst **DIY** memory

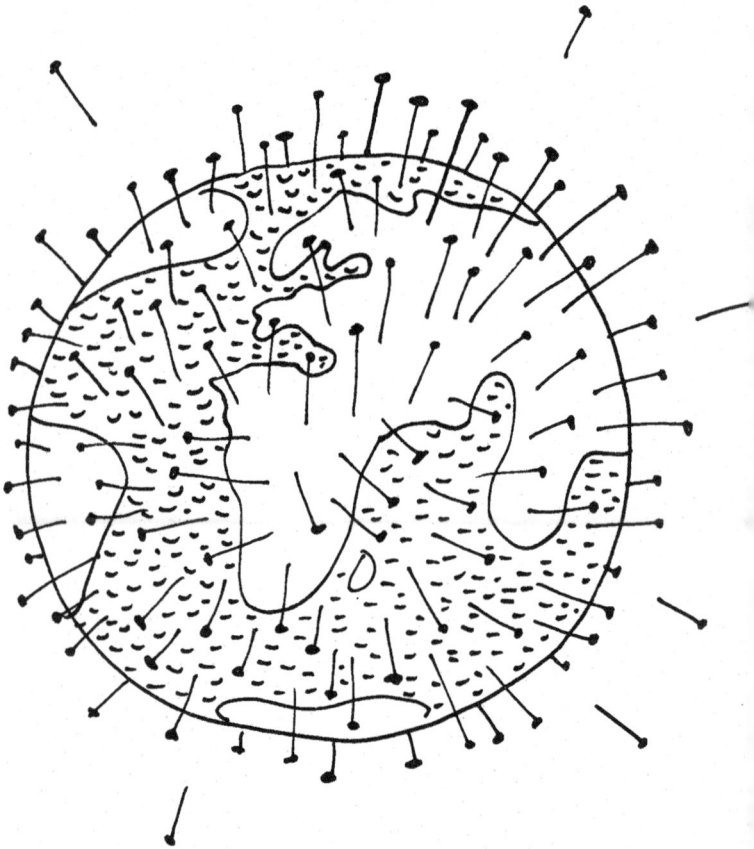

FIND

# THE BAD IN THE WORLD

What ruins **WORK?**

What ruins *a meal*?

What ruins a **road trip**?

What ruins A BUS RIDE?

What ruins a *flight*?

What ruins a visit to a restaurant?

What ruins A MOVIE?

What ruins a TRIP TO THE SUPERMARKET?

What ruins a *trip to the doctor*?

What ruins a **NIGHT IN**?

What ruins a **TV SHOW**?

What ruins a **BOOK**?

What ruins a **FEW DAYS OFF FROM WORK**?

What ruins a *vacation*?

What ruins a **party**?

What ruins a **WORKOUT**?

What's most irritating in **THE CITY**?

What's most irritating in **THE COUNTRY**?

What's most irritating **ABOUT THE GOVERNMENT**?

What's most irritating in **NEWSPAPERS**?

What's most irritating on **TV**?

What's most irritating about **SOCIETY**?

What's the most irritating **LAW**?

What's most annoying about **kids**?

What's most annoying about **TEENAGERS**?

What's most annoying about *adults*?

What's most annoying about **THE ELDERLY**?

What's most annoying about **ANIMALS**?

What's most annoying about **you**?

What's most annoying about **this book**?

My least favorite candy is...

My least favorite food is...

My least favorite drink is...

The most pointless tourist attraction is...

The stupidest form of entertainment is...

The worst music is...

The worst chore is...

The dumbest kind of exercise is...

The most ridiculous piece of clothing is...

The most pointless status symbol is...

**DRAW SOMETHING STUPID AND POINTLESS**

The most pointless invention is...

The most pointless pastime is...

The most pointless profession is...

The most pointless animal is...

The most pointless saying is...

The most pointless conversation topic is...

The biggest waste of money is...

It's gauche to...

It's ridiculous to...

It's childish to...

It's rude to...

It's beyond the pale to...

It's unforgivable to...

It's overrated to...

List all the ACHES and PAINS you've suffered from, suffer from now, or fear you may suffer from in the future.

# BADDEN YOUR VOCABULARY

**IRRITATING**, *annoying*, **INFURIATING**...

Continue the list!

# IDIOT, numbskull, *twit*...

Continue the list!

write **swear words** and **insults** in different handwriting.

*Why don't you go...*

Eat...

write the swear words you know
in a foreign language.

Which trendy
hate?

What words/p
a snob?

Which rude wo
most repulsive

Stupidest old s

## Words only ever used by

### REDNECKS

### SNOBS

### TEENAGE BRATS

### OLD FOSSILS

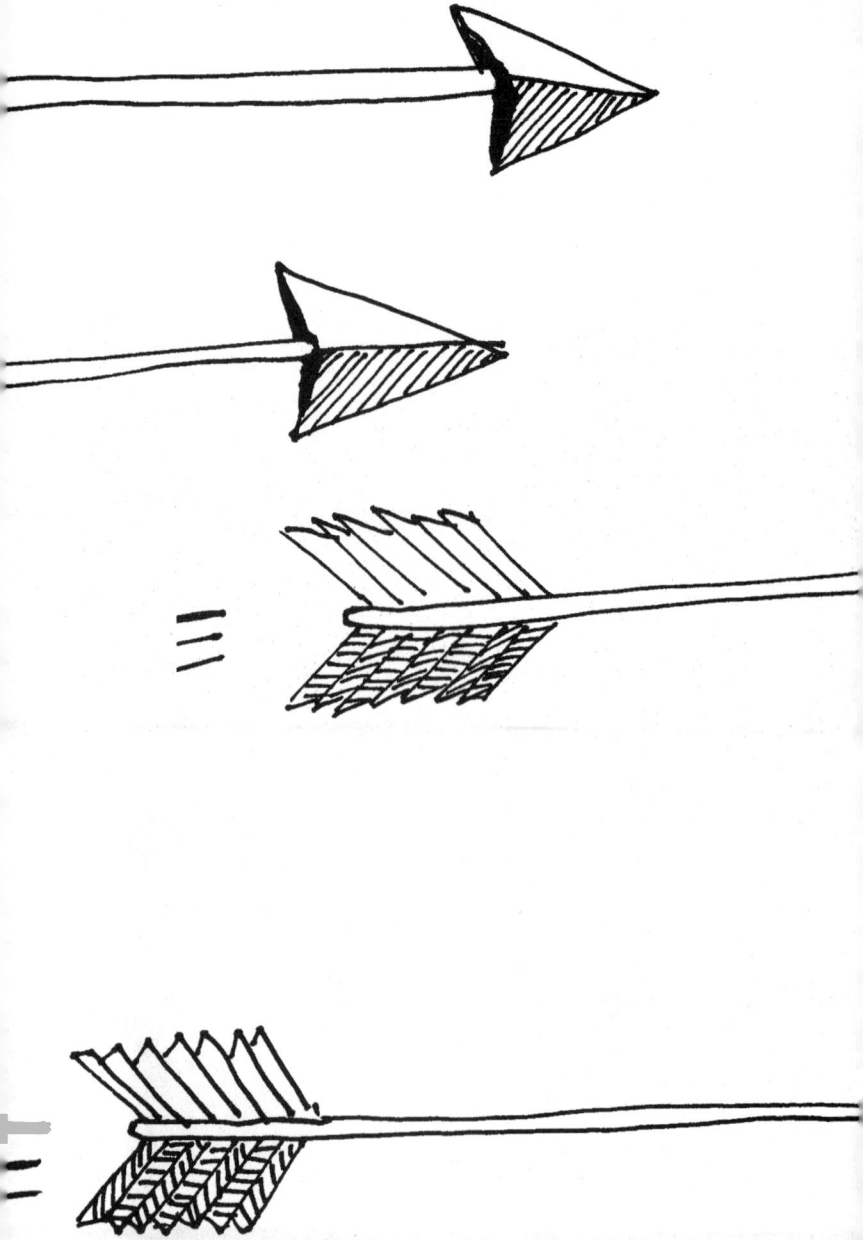

# JUST SAY IT ALREADY

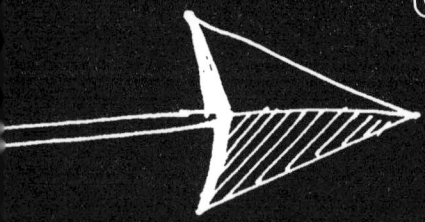

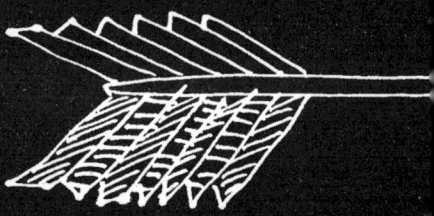

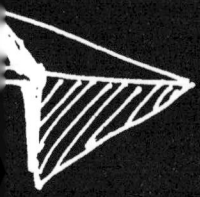

Most people don't understand these simple things:

Name four people you'd like to

# TELL OFF.

USE THE SPEECH BUBBLES TO GIVE THEM A PIECE OF YOUR MIND.

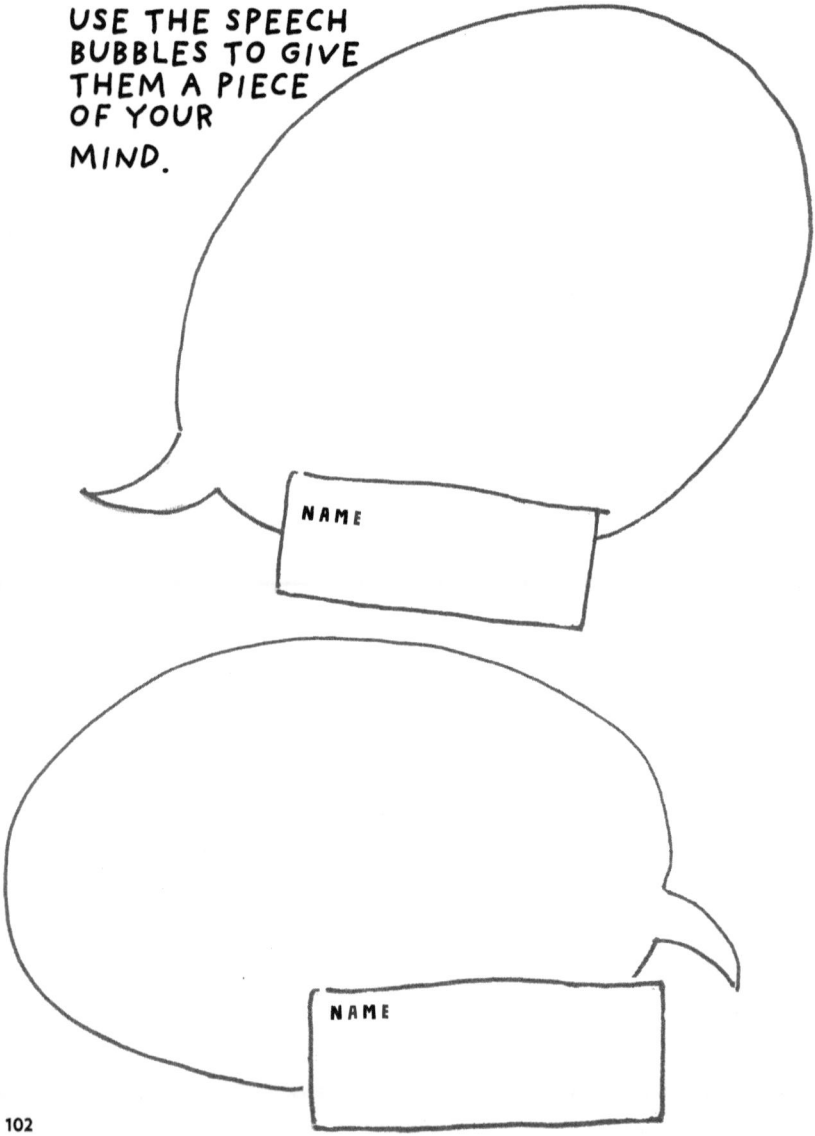

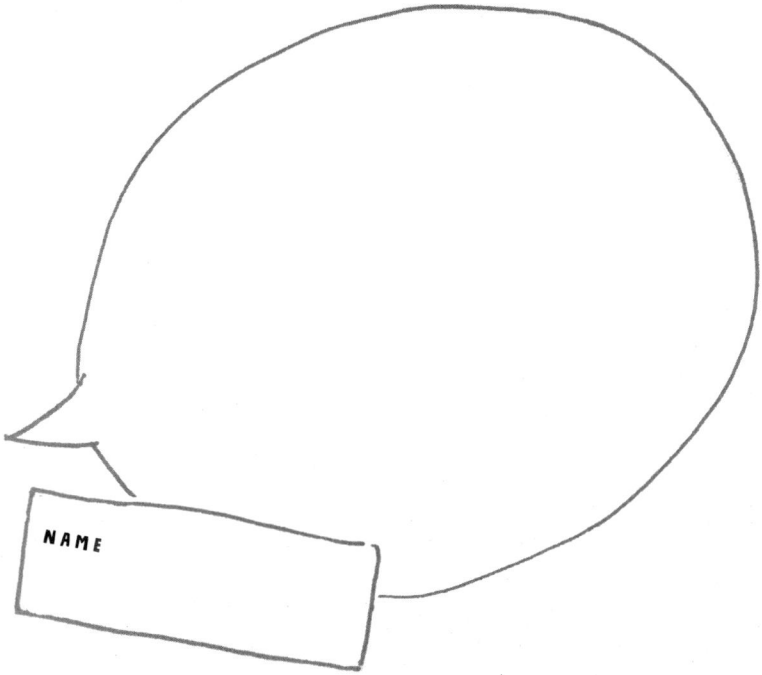
NAME

NAME

Write your irritating neighbor A NASTY NOTE.

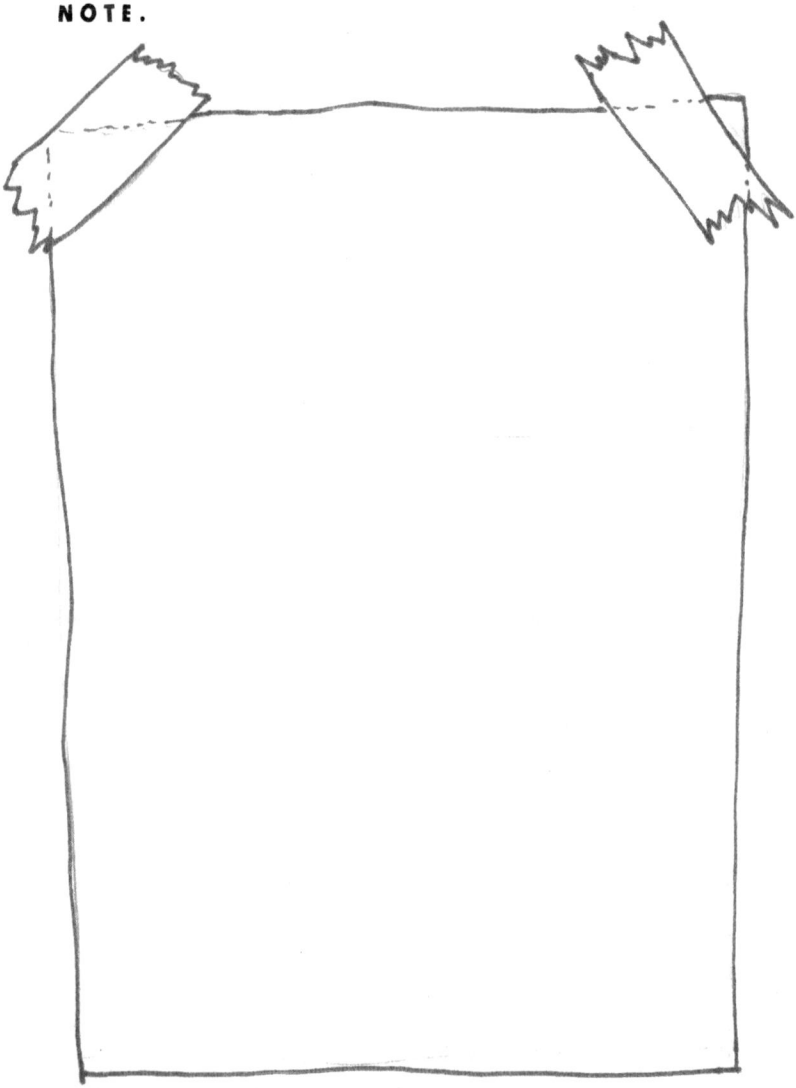

Write a message to your former teacher you **STILL HATE**.

Write a message to a salesperson/waiter/ etc. **who insulted you forever ago.**

Write a message to your EX you still think is a jerk.

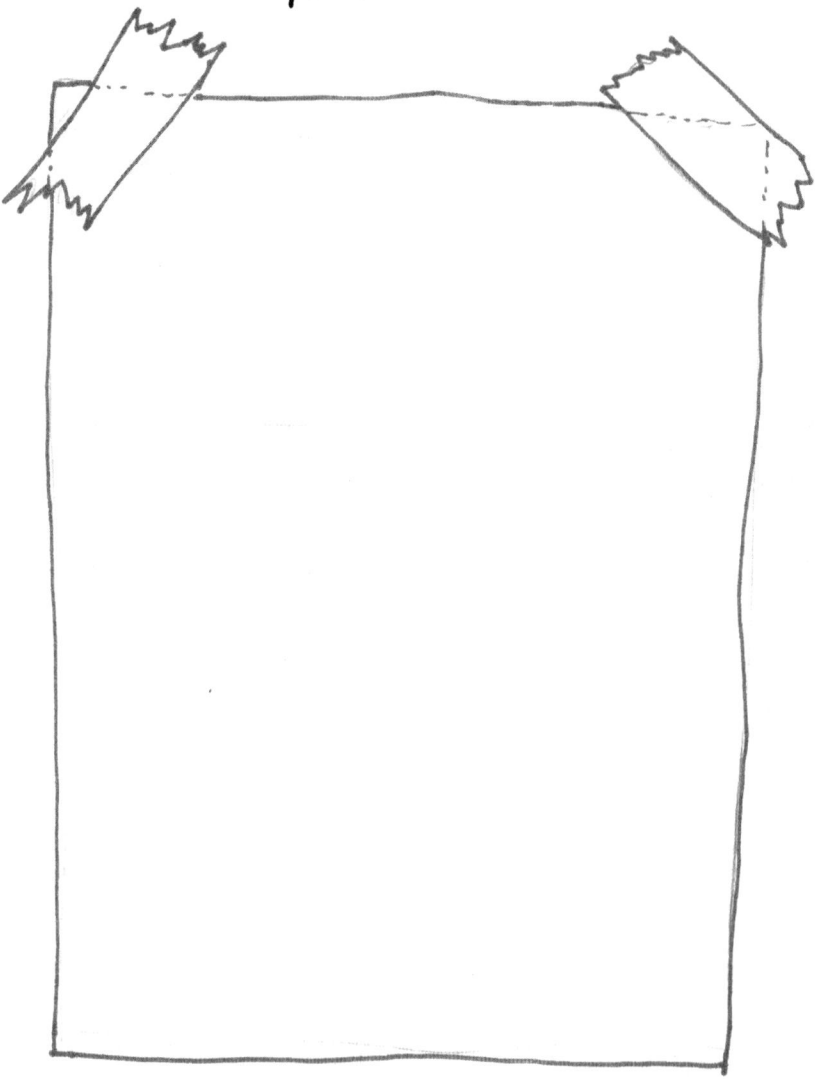

LIVE
LOVE
LEARN

# COLOR ME BAD

Design or write **the most idiotic decorative thing** to hang on a wall.

Color the **half-empty glasses.**

Color.

Write or draw and color
**the most irritating slogan.**

Draw and write greetings from

# disaster holidays!

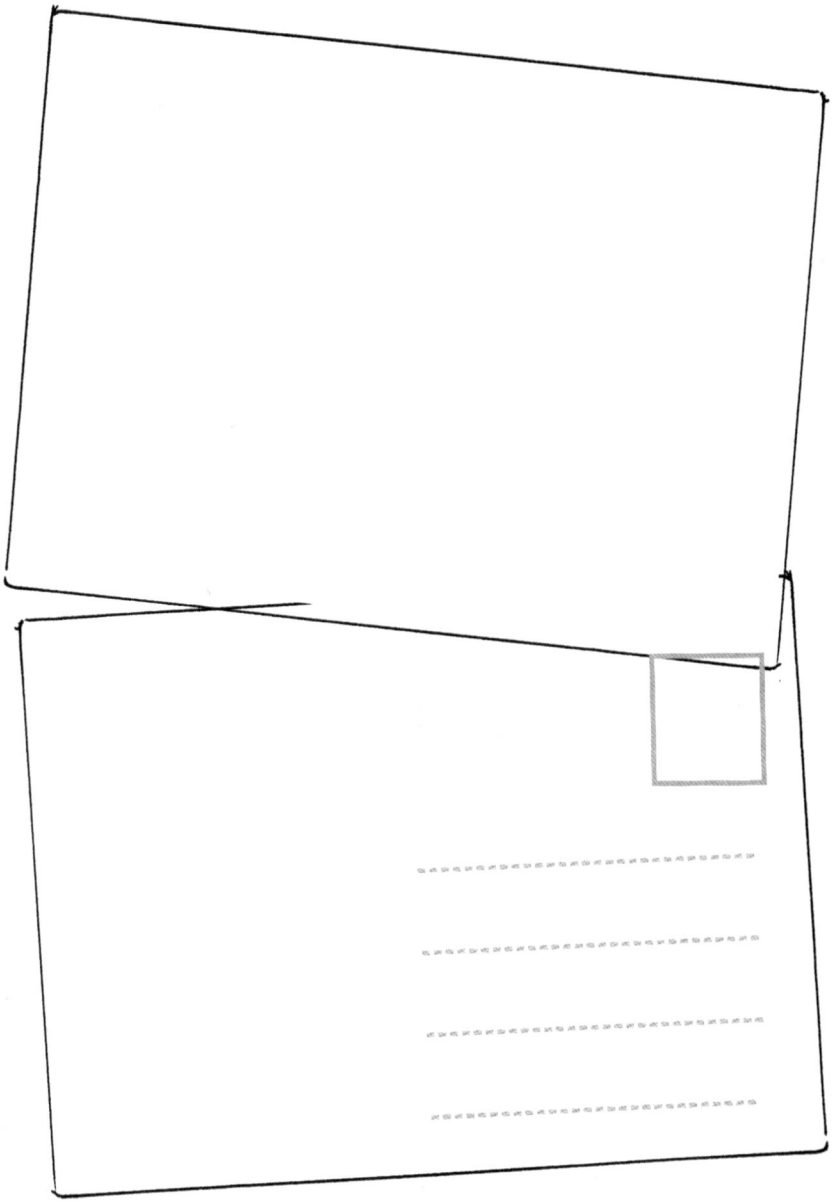

Name the circles and color the diagram.

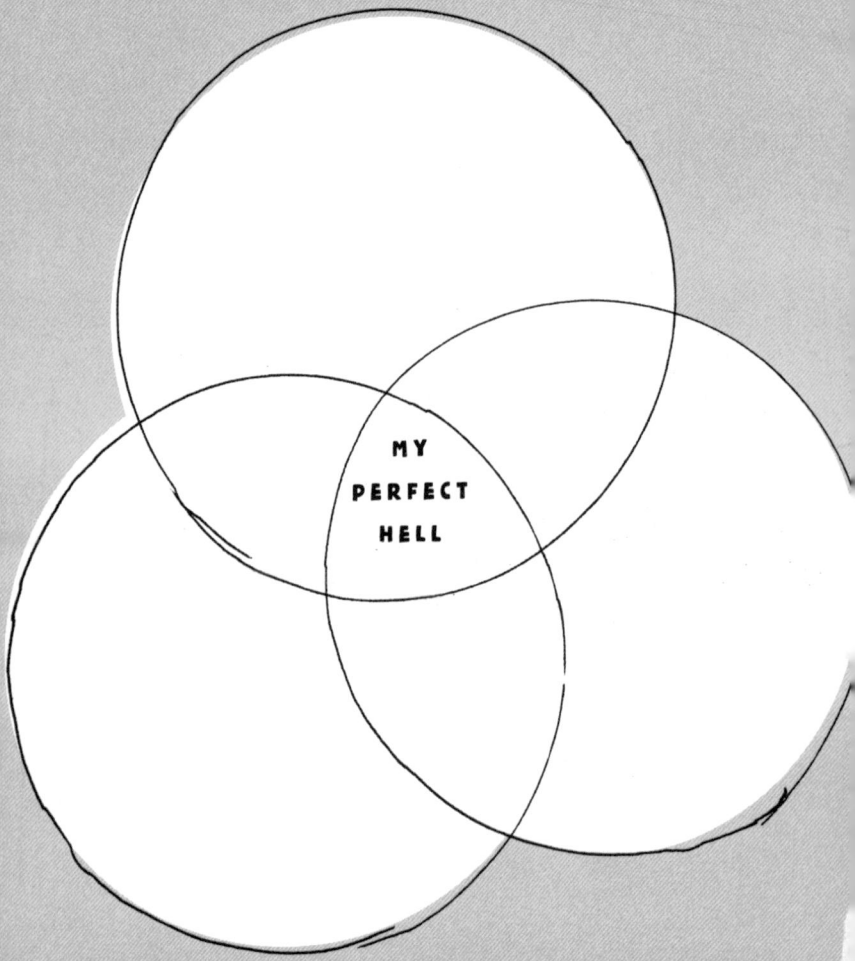

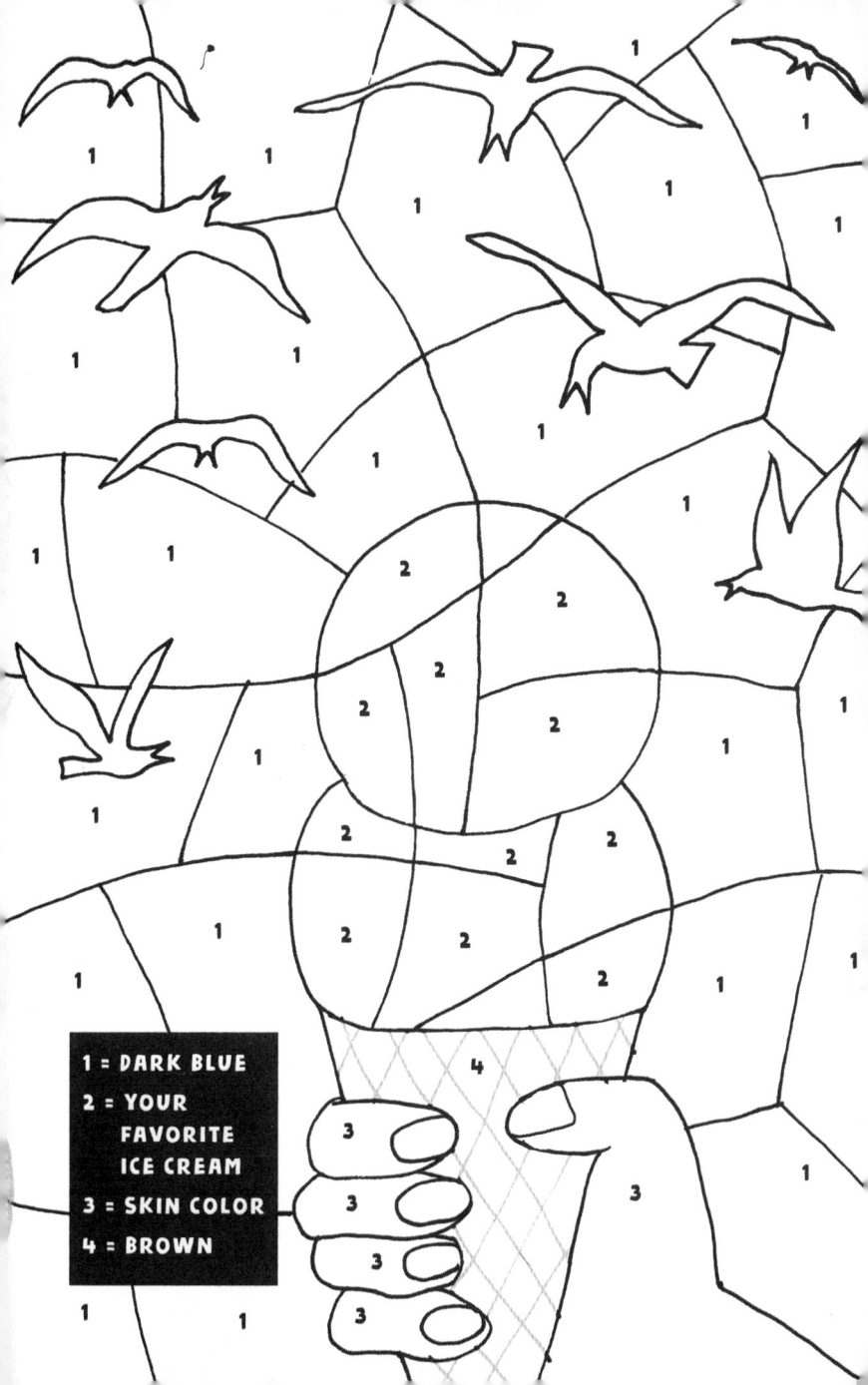
1 = DARK BLUE
2 = YOUR FAVORITE ICE CREAM
3 = SKIN COLOR
4 = BROWN

# FORECAST IS DISMAL

## I HATE

- ☐ Public transportation
- ☐ Drivers
- ☐ Pedestrians
- ☐ Bikers
- ☐ _____

BECAUSE_____

_____

## I HATE

- ☐ Spring
- ☐ Summer
- ☐ Fall
- ☐ Winter
- ☐ _____

BECAUSE_____

_____

## I HATE

- ☐ Ski jumping
- ☐ Ice hockey
- ☐ Football
- ☐ Javelin throwing
- ☐ _____

BECAUSE_____

_____

## I HATE

- ☐ Christmas
- ☐ Fourth of July
- ☐ Valentine's Day
- ☐ Easter
- ☐ _____

BECAUSE_____

_____

## I HATE

- ☐ Buying clothes
- ☐ Buying shoes
- ☐ Buying cars
- ☐ Buying computers
- ☐ _____

BECAUSE_____

_____

## I HATE

- ☐ Dogs
- ☐ Cats
- ☐ Guinea pigs
- ☐ Pet owners
- ☐ _____

BECAUSE_____

_____

## I HATE

- ☐ Heavy metal
- ☐ Rap
- ☐ Country
- ☐ Pop
- ☐ Classical
- ☐ _____

BECAUSE_____

_____

## I HATE

- ☐ Soup
- ☐ Fish
- ☐ Pudding
- ☐ Veal
- ☐ _____

BECAUSE_____

_____

## AT SCHOOL I HATED

- ☐ Art
- ☐ P.E.
- ☐ Math
- ☐ Home economics
- ☐ _____

BECAUSE_____

_____

## I HATE

- ☐ Leggings
- ☐ Pantyhose
- ☐ Dress shirts
- ☐ Sweats
- ☐ _____

BECAUSE_____

_____

## I HATE

- ☐ Vacuuming
- ☐ Cleaning dishes
- ☐ Washing windows
- ☐ Ironing
- ☐ _____

BECAUSE_____

_____

## I HATE

- ☐ Plumbing
- ☐ Yard work
- ☐ Community meetings
- ☐ Neighbors
- ☐ _____

BECAUSE_____

_____

## I HATE

- ☐ _____
- ☐ _____
- ☐ _____
- ☐ _____
- ☐ _____

BECAUSE_____

_____

Have a bad day!